# 101+ Ways To Keep A Man

# 101+ Ways To Keep A Man

*By Jeff Hodge & Denver Williams*

iUniverse, Inc.
New York Lincoln Shanghai

# 101+ Ways To Keep A Man

iUniverse books may be ordered through booksellers or by contacting:

iUniverse
2021 Pine Lake Road, Suite 100
Lincoln, NE 68512
www.iuniverse.com
1-800-Authors (1-800-288-4677)


First Edition
Text © 2005 by Jeff Hodge & Denver Williams
Jokes © Anonymous Authors
Illustrations © Angel D'Amico


ISBN-13: 978-0-595-37633-9 (pbk)
ISBN-13: 978-0-595-82024-5 (ebk)
ISBN-10: 0-595-37633-9 (pbk)
ISBN-10: 0-595-82024-7 (ebk)

Printed in the United States of America

This book is dedicated to all the single, lonely women out there searching for love. Keep the faith, and may God continue to bless you in your search for that perfect mate.

# Contents

# Acknowledgments

Thanks:                      To M. Collins, Sattiewhite, Beth Ann Meyers, Lauren "Bro. Wack" Gumbs, Gerry "Mr. Bangladesh" Bednob, and Romona Carter.

Special Thanks:              To all the women we've dated in our lives for giving us all the material for this book.

Extra Special Thanks: To the Hodge and Williams families. Thanks for all your love and support throughout the years.

Big Shout-Outs:              To Francis "Big Fran" Acquaye, Kelvin "Wobbly" Hodge, Willis Turner, Trent Brisco, Khari Wyatt, Jackie Rachal, Edgar Hodge, Dawn Williams and "Jamming" Wayne Williams up in Toronto. Ambassadors of Comedy, thanks for all the jokes. You guys are too funny (www.ambassadorsofcomedy.com).

# *Introduction*

Finally, an inspirational book that gives women practical advice on how to coexist with the male species. For many years, Denver and I have dispensed free advice about men and what makes them tick to the many women whom we have encountered in our daily lives.

I recently went on a cruise, Festival at Sea, sponsored by Blue World Travel, and I overheard so many women talking about finding a husband or a good man that Denver and I decided to write this book.

The advice written here is not clinical advice; that is because neither of us is a psychologist, doctor, or therapist. We are just a couple of regular guys who have been around the block a few times. We have been in countless relationships over the years and have interviewed hundreds of guys to come up with this list of things men like and don't like about the women with whom they are involved.

The advice contained in this book is simple, everyday advice most men sit around and talk about with their buddies all the time. What we noticed about women is they do not seem to understand how easy it is to get and keep a man. Women tend to make men out to be more complicated than we really are. Men are simple. All we want is food, sex, and sleep. Everything else is gravy.

Ladies, the bottom line is this: a man wants to feel appreciated. It doesn't matter how attractive you are or how good the sex is; if your man doesn't feel that you appreciate him, he will look elsewhere for appreciation.

We hope that after reading this book, a light bulb will turn on inside your head and make things easier for you to understand men. Most important, this book should help women better understand how men think and should give them a better perspective of how to be a good mate and deal with any man in their lives.

Also, because I (Jeff) am a comedian, I've decided to keep the mood light in this book by including some of my favorite street jokes that I have heard or read over the years. All the jokes are relationship related, so they make the book entertaining as well as informative.

**1. Don't ask questions you really don't want to know the answers to.** *("Do I look fat in this dress?" is an argument waiting to happen. If you have to ask the question, you probably are!)*

**2. Don't be a ho!** *(This is self-explanatory.)*

**3. Don't have sex with his friends.** *(We can forgive you for sleeping with the bellman in Cancun, but not our best friend.)*

**4. Don't have sex with his family members.** *(That old saying about not eating where you shit applies here.)*

# _The Geography of a Man_

Between fifteen and seventy,

A man is like Libya—

ruled by a dick.

**5. Quit bitching and shut the hell up!** *(Silence really is golden. You can enjoy each other quietly.)*

**6. Don't keep pictures of you and your ex around the house where your man can find them.** *(Especially if you happen to be naked in the photos.)*

**7. Never use sex as a weapon.** *(It just might backfire on you.)*

**8. Visit your gynecologist *regularly*!** *(Fish is the only thing that should smell like fish.)*

## My Brains

A three-year-old little boy was examining his testicles while taking a bath. "Mama," he asked, "are these my brains?" Mama answered, "*Not yet!*"

## Mother of Six

A man has six children and is very proud of his achievement. He is so proud of himself that he starts calling his wife "Mother of Six" in spite of her objections. One night, they go to a party. The man decides that it's time to go home and wants to find out if his wife is ready to leave as well. He shouts at the top of his voice, "Shall we go home, Mother of Six?" His wife, irritated by her husband's lack of discretion, shouts right back, "Anytime you're ready, 'Father of Four.'"

**9. Learn to give massages.** *(If you don't do it, some other female will.)*

**10. Don't ever call his mother a bitch.** *(You have to give respect to get respect.)*

**11. Initiate sex.** *(Sex should be fun, not work.)*

**12. Take a bath regularly.** *(Perfume doesn't cover up all odors.)*

Top Ten Things Men Understand About Women

1.

2.

3.

4.

5.

6.

7.

8.

9.

10.

**13. Go to the dentist.** *(Nothing turns a guy off more than a woman with a jacked-up grill.)*

**14. Give him lots of sex.** *(In the history of mankind, no man has ever left his woman because he was getting too much sex.)*

**15. Don't leave your underwear in his bed when you go back to your house.** *(If he wants a pair of your underwear as a souvenir, he will ask you for it.)*

**16. Be flexible and spontaneous with your sex life.** *(If time only allows for a quickie, do it and quit holding out for foreplay.)*

## <u>*Women's Ass Size Study*</u>

Here is a new study about women and how they feel about their asses!

85% of women think their ass is too big...

10% of women think their ass is too little...

The other 5% say that they don't care, they love him, he's a good man, and they would have married him anyway.

**17. Give him oral sex. And still *more* oral sex.** *(Being a champ at fellatio will earn you lots of brownie points.)*

**18. Lose some weight and stay in shape.** *(Men are physical creatures, so looks mean everything. Remember that there is a lot of eye candy out there for your man to look at.)*

**19. It may sound unfair, but guys don't want to know when you have to go to the bathroom to do a Number 2.** *(You're much too beautiful for that.)*

**20. If you've since changed your ways, don't tell your man how wild and freaky you *used* to be.** *(He wants to get what the last guy got and more.)*

# Sheer Lingerie

A husband walks into Frederick's of Hollywood to purchase some sheer lingerie for his wife. He is shown several possibilities that range from $250 to $500; the more sheer the lingerie is, the higher the price.

He opts for the sheerest item, pays the $500, and takes the lingerie home. He presents it to his wife and asks her to go upstairs, put it on, and model it for him.

Upstairs, the wife thinks, "I have an idea. It's so sheer that it might as well be nothing. I won't put it on, and I'll do the modeling naked, return it tomorrow, and keep the $500 refund for myself."

So she appears naked on the balcony and strikes a pose. The husband says, "Good Lord! You'd think that for $500, they'd at least iron it!"

He never heard the shot. Funeral services are pending.

**21. When he says leave him alone, leave him alone!** *(He's not joking.)*

**22. Lose the attitude and be pleasant.** *(Like that old saying goes, "You can catch more flies with honey than with vinegar.")*

**23. Let your man go to the strip club a few times a year.** *(Going to a strip club for a guy is like a woman going shopping—just innocent fun.)*

**24. Don't be a stalker.** *(Stalking him isn't going to bring him back. If anything, he will want to get farther away from you.)*

# Four Men

Four men went golfing one day. Three of them headed to the first tee, and the fourth went into the clubhouse to take care of the bill. The three men started talking and bragging about their sons.

The first man told the others, "My son is a home builder, and he is so successful that he gave a friend a new home for free. Just gave it to him!"

The second man said, "My son was a car salesman, and now he owns a multi-line dealership. He's so successful that he gave one of his friends a new Mercedes, fully loaded."

The third man, not wanting to be outdone, bragged, "My son is a stockbroker, and he's doing so well that he gave his friend an entire portfolio."

The fourth man joined them on the tee after a few minutes of taking care of business. The first man mentioned, "We were just talking about our sons. How is yours doing?" The fourth man replied, "Well, my son is gay and go-go dances in a gay bar."

The other three men grew silent as he continued, "I'm not totally thrilled about the dancing job, but he must be doing well. His last three boyfriends gave him a house, a brand new Mercedes, and a stock portfolio."

**25. Don't do any complaining in the first thirty minutes after you both arrive at home.** *(Nobody likes a nag, so don't do it.)*

**26. No baby daddy drama.** *(Keep all problems with the father of your kids away from your current relationship. Men are very territorial.)*

**27. Seek therapy when needed.** *(Constantly using issues from the past to explain erratic behavior gets old really fast.)*

**28. Don't give him a list.** *(This is the surest way to get kicked to the curb.)*

# An example of a list not to give to your man:

A.  *You have to take me out dancing once a week.*

B.  *You must take me shopping every weekend.*

C.  *I have to be taken out to dinner a couple of times a month.*

D.  *When you get paid, be sure to give me your paycheck.*

E.  *There is no watching sports when I'm at home.*

F.  *We must have sex twice a week, only on the weekends, and only if I feel like it.*

G.  *I absolutely do not "give head."*

## KY Jelly

My husband came home with a tube of KY jelly and said, "This will make you happy tonight." He was right. When he went out of the bedroom, I squirted it all over the doorknobs. He couldn't get back in.

## Happy Woman

A couple is lying in bed. The man says, "I am going to make you the happiest woman in the world." The woman says, "I'll miss you."

## Macho Computer

A female computer consultant was helping this macho-type guy set up his computer. When she got to the preference setup, she asked him for a password. Attempting to embarrass the pretty female, he told her to enter "penis."

Without blinking or making any response, she entered the password. She almost died laughing at the computer's quick response:

"Password rejected. Not long enough."

**29. Discuss personal problems about him with him, not your girlfriends.** *(This is like adding gasoline to a fire. Only you and he can fix the problem, so why invite trouble into your relationship?)*

**30. Never feel like it's ever okay to hit your man.** *(Contrary to popular belief, men do feel pain.)*

**31. Learn something about his favorite sports.** *(There are plenty of other women out there who would love to attend a game or two with your man because you're "not into sports.")*

**32. Make and have your own money!** *(Nobody likes a moocher or gold digger.)*

# Confounded Sex

A man was in a terrible accident, and his penis was mangled and torn from his body. His doctor assured him that modern medicine could give him back his manhood, but that his insurance wouldn't cover the surgery, because it was considered cosmetic. The doctor said the cost would be $3,500 for "small," $6,500 for "medium," and $14,000 for "large."

The man was sure he would want a medium or large, but the doctor urged him to talk it over with his wife before he made any decision. The man called his wife on the phone and explained their options. The doctor came back into the room and found the man looking dejected. "Well, what have the two of you decided?" asked the doctor. The man answered, "She'd rather remodel the kitchen."

**33. Be independent. Don't count on a man to take care of you.** *(Men like women who can hold down the fort when they are sick or away for any period of time.)*

**34. Don't try to change him.** *(If you don't like who he is, then find someone else. Only a man can change himself.)*

**35. Don't take relationship advice from any female who doesn't have a man, can't get a man, or can't keep a man.** *(There are a lot of haters out there, so buyer beware!)*

**36. Quit dressing like a "hootchie mamma," especially if you are older than thirty-five.** *(Guys want a slut in the bedroom and a lady in public.)*

## Quiet Sex

Tired of a listless sex life, the man came right out and asked his wife during a recent lovemaking session, "How come you never tell me when you have an orgasm?" She glanced at him casually and replied, "You're never home!"

## Loud Sex

A wife went to see a therapist and said, "I've got a big problem, doctor. Every time we're in bed and my husband climaxes, he lets out this ear-splitting yell." "My dear," the shrink said, "that's completely natural. I don't see what the problem is." "The problem is," she complained, "it wakes me up!"

**37. Don't play mind games.** *(This is so high school. Games are for kids.)*

**38. Don't try to control him.** *(Let a man be a man.)*

**39. Make better choices.** *(If you keep meeting assholes, change what you are doing and where you're looking for a man.)*

**40. Pick your battles. Every disagreement doesn't have to be a war.** *(If your man treats you right and is a good guy, don't complain about the toilet seat being up.)*

## Jamaican Firefighter

A newlywed Jamaican fireman came home from work one day and said to his wife: "Y'know sumptin, honey, we have a wonderful system at de fire station. Bell 1 rings—we put on we jackets. Bell 2 rings—we slide down de pole. Bell 3 rings—we jump on de engine and we's ready to go.

"From now on, when I say 'Bell 1,' I want you to strip naked. When I say 'Bell 2,' you jump on de bed. When I say 'Bell 3,' we gonna mek love all tru de night."

The next night, he came home and shouted: "Bell 1," and she stripped naked; "Bell 2," and she jumped on the bed; "Bell 3," and they started to make love.

After a few minutes, the wife yelled out "Bell 4!"

"What de hell is Bell 4, woman?"

She replied: "It means roll out more hose, man, you ain't nowhere near de fire."

**41. Agree to disagree.** *(You're not always going to agree on everything. The sooner you understand this, the better your relationship will be.)*

**42. Don't give him ultimatums.** *(Unless you are willing to live with the consequences if he calls you on your bluff, don't do this. Men hate to be told what to do.)*

**43. Don't be a lush.** *(At least not in public.)*

**44. Appreciate the gifts that he gives you even if you don't like them.** *(If you show your appreciation, the gifts will keep coming, and he's bound to get it right sooner or later.)*

# Perfect Evening

Jenny's husband, Charley, was a male chauvinist. Even though they both worked full-time, he never helped around the house. Housework was woman's work! But one evening, Jenny arrived home from work to find the children bathed, one load of clothes in the washer and another in the dryer, dinner on the stove, and the table set. She was astonished; something was up.

It turned out that Charley had read an article that said wives who worked full-time and had to do their own housework were too tired to have sex.

The night went well, and the next day she told her office friends all about it. "We had a great dinner. Charley even cleaned up. He helped the kids do their homework, folded all the laundry, and put everything away. I really enjoyed the evening."

"But what about afterward?" asked her friends.

"Oh, that was perfect too. Charley was too tired!"

**45. Don't go looking for problems unless you can deal with them once you've found them.** *(Asking him about the threesome he had with his former girlfriend and her best friend is an argument waiting to happen.)*

**46. Listen to what he says and stop trying to hear what you want to hear.** *(If he tells you that he's not looking for a commitment, that's what he means. It doesn't mean, "He's not looking for a commitment today. You can change his mind tomorrow.")*

**47. Don't show up with your girls at Boys Night Out.** *(It's called Boy's Night Out for a reason.)*

**48. Don't do tit for tat.** *(If he stays out late one night without calling and saying where he is, do not turn around and do the same thing the following night.)*

## Marriage

A man and a woman who have never met before find themselves assigned to the same sleeping room on a transcontinental train. Though initially embarrassed and uneasy over sharing a room, the two are tired and fall asleep quickly, he in the upper bunk and she in the lower.

At 1:00 AM, the man leans over and gently awakens the woman, saying, "Miss, I'm sorry to bother you, but would you be willing to reach into the closet to get me a second blanket? It's very cold."

"I have a better idea," she replies. "Just for tonight, why don't we pretend we're married?"

"Wow, sure!" he exclaims. "That's a great idea!"

"Good," she replies. "Get your own damn blanket."

**49. Don't create drama.** *(A relationship should be harmonious, not constant fighting and arguing.)*

**50. Don't be superficial.** *(Nothing is as unattractive as a woman who is out for material possessions, money, etc.)*

**51. Don't be selfish.** *(A relationship is a two-way street, a partnership.)*

**52. Don't be a bitch!** *(Again, this is self-explanatory.)*

# The Good Wife

A husband should always be able to count on his wife. There was a man who had worked all of his life and had saved everything he made, and he was really tight when it came to his money.

He loved money more than just about anything, and just before he died, he said to his wife, "Now listen. When I die, I want you to take all my money and put it in the casket with me. I want to take my money to the afterlife with me." And so he got his wife to promise him with all of her heart that when he died, she would put all of the money in the casket with him.

Well, he died. He was stretched out in the casket, his wife was sitting there in black, and her dearest friend was sitting next to her. When they finished the ceremony, just before the undertakers got ready to close the casket, the wife said, "Wait a minute!" She had a box with her; she came over with the box and put it in the casket. Then the undertakers locked the casket down, and they rolled it away.

Her friend said, "Girl, I know you weren't fool enough to put all that money in there with your husband."

"Listen, I'm a good woman; I can't go back on my word. I promised him with all my heart that I was gonna put that money in that casket with him."

"You mean to tell me you really put all that money in the casket with him?"

"I sure did," said the wife. "I wrote him a check."

**53. Your sex life is your sex life.** *(Don't share everything about your sex life with your nosey girlfriends.)*

**54. Do not insult him in public or mixed company.** *(Men are driven by ego. You crush it, and you take away his reason to be with you.)*

**55. Don't compare!** *(Past relationships, another man, your sex life, or anything for that matter, to your man, especially not in his presence.)*

**56. Don't instigate arguments or problems.** *(Nobody likes a drama queen, so quit with all the mess.)*

# CIA

The CIA had an opening for an assassin. After all the background checks, interviews, and testing were done, there were three finalists—two men and a woman.

For the final test, the CIA agents took one of the men to a large metal door and handed him a gun. "We must know that you will follow your instructions, no matter what the circumstances. Inside this room, you will find your wife sitting in a chair. Kill her."

The man said, "You can't be serious. I could never shoot my wife." The agent said, "Then you're not the right man for this job. Take your wife and go home."

The second man was given the same instructions. He took the gun and went into the room. All was quiet for about five minutes. Then the man came out with tears in his eyes. "I tried, but I can't kill my wife." The agent said, "You don't have what it takes. Take your wife and go home."

Finally, it was the woman's turn. She was given the instruction to kill her husband. She took the gun and went into the room. The agent heard shots, one after another. He heard screaming, crashing, and banging on the walls. After a few minutes, all was quiet. The door opened slowly, and there stood the woman. She wiped the sweat from her brow. "This gun was loaded with blanks," she said. "I had to beat him to death with the chair."

**57. Be supportive of his dreams.** *(If they are legal.)*

**58. Let go of the past.** *(What happened in the past should stay in the past.)*

**59. Don't tell your man how much the last guy you dated mistreated you and then give him no slack when he makes a tiny mistake.** *(Treat him as you would like to be treated.)*

**60. Stop listening to your girlfriends' exaggerated stories about how much better their love life is than yours.** *(Watch your enemies, but watch your jealous girlfriends even closer. They are usually up to no good.)*

# Honeymoon

A young couple got married and went on their honeymoon. When they got back, the bride immediately called her mother. "Well," said her mother, "how was the honeymoon?"

"Oh, Mama," she replied, "The honeymoon was wonderful! So romantic..." Suddenly she burst out crying. "But, Mama, as soon as we returned, Sam started using the most horrible language—things I'd never heard before! I mean, all these awful four-letter words! You've got to take me home, please Mama!"

"Sarah, Sarah," her mother said, "calm down! You need to stay with your husband and work this out. Now, tell me, what could be so awful? *What* four-letter words?"

"Please don't make me tell you, Mama," wept the daughter. "I'm so embarrassed, they're just too awful! Come get me, please!"

"Baby, you must tell me what has you so upset. Tell your mother these horrible four-letter words!"

Still sobbing, the bride said, "Oh, Mama, he used words like dust, wash, iron, cook..."

The mother replied, "I'll pick you up in twenty minutes!"

**61. Mind your own business.** *(Nothing is worse than a woman who is always meddling in other people's affairs.)*

**62. Respect him.** *(Make him feel appreciated.)*

**63. Have some self-respect.** *(If you don't respect yourself, don't expect him to respect you either.)*

**64. Tell him what the hell you want; don't drop subtle hints.** *(Contrary to what you might think, a guy can't read your mind. Don't expect him to spend his entire day thinking about what you want.)*

## Are You the Manager?

A very attractive lady approaches the bar in a quiet neighborhood pub. She gestures invitingly to the bartender, who comes over immediately. When he arrives, she seductively signals that he should bring his face closer to hers.

When he does, she begins to gently caress his full beard. "Are you the manager?" she asks, softly stroking his face with both hands.

"Actually, no," the man replied.

"Can you get him for me? I need to speak to him," she says, running her hands beyond his beard and into his hair.

"I'm afraid I can't," breathes the bartender. "Is there anything I can do?"

"Yes, there is. I need you to give him a message," she continues running her forefinger across the bartender's lips and slyly popping a couple of her fingers into his mouth and allowing him to suck them gently.

"What should I tell him?" the bartender manages to ask.

"Tell him," she whispers, "there is no toilet paper, hand soap, or paper towels in the ladies room."

**65. Get a life.** *(There is more to life than shopping and watching reality shows or soap operas.)*

**66. Remember, he is not the last man you dated.** *(He shouldn't have to pay for the actions of your previous man.)*

**67. Encourage your man to hang out with his buddies.** *(Male bonding is essential to a man's peace of mind.)*

**68. Stop speaking to your man like he is your child.** *(This is another quick way to turn your man off.)*

# Pig

A man drives down a road, tra la la, just driving along. A woman drives down the road from the opposite direction. As they pass each other, the woman leans out the window and yells, "*Pig!*"

The man immediately leans out of his window and yells, "*Bitch!*" As the man rounds the next curve, he crashes into a huge pig in the middle of the road and dies.

# An Orgasm

A man and a woman are sitting beside each other in the first-class section of the plane. The woman sneezes, takes a tissue, gently wipes her nose, and shudders violently in her seat.

The man isn't sure why she is shuddering and goes back to reading. A few minutes pass. The woman sneezes again. She takes a tissue, gently wipes her nose, and shudders quite violently in her seat. The man is becoming more and more curious about the shuddering. A few more minutes pass. The woman sneezes yet again. She takes a tissue, gently wipes her nose, and shudders violently again.

The man has finally had all he can handle. He turns to the woman and says, "Three times you've sneezed, and three times you've taken a tissue and wiped your nose then shuddered violently! Do you want me to call the stewardess for you?"

The woman replies, "I'm sorry if I disturbed you. I have a rare condition, and when I sneeze, I have an orgasm."

The man, now feeling a little embarrassed but even more curious says, "I've never heard of that before. What are you taking for it?"

The woman looks at him and says, "Pepper."

**69. When he's home, limit your phone conversations to twenty minutes or less.** *(Everyone likes attention, so give it to him when he is home.)*

**70. Go out with him at least once a week.** *(Have a date night for just the two of you.)*

**71. If you ask a question, don't throw a fit if you don't like the answer.** *(Sometimes the truth hurts, so deal with it.)*

**72. Don't do drive-bys at his residence.** *(Insecurity in a relationship is not good.)*

# The Ostrich

A man walks into a restaurant with a full-grown ostrich behind him, and as he sits, the waitress comes over and asks for their order. The man says, "I'll have a hamburger, fries, and a Coke," and turns to the ostrich. "What's yours?"

"I'll have the same," says the ostrich.

A short time later, the waitress returns with the order. "That will be $6.40 please," and the man reaches into his pocket and pulls out exact change for payment.

The next day, the man and the ostrich come in again, and the man says, "I'll have a hamburger, fries, and a Coke," and the ostrich says, "I'll have the same." Once again the man reaches into his pocket and pays with exact change.

This becomes a routine until late one evening, the two enter again. "The usual?" asks the waitress.

"No, this is Friday night, so I'll have a steak, baked potato, and salad," says the man.

"Same for me," says the ostrich.

A short time later, the waitress comes with the order and says, "That will be $12.62." Once again, the man pulls exact change out of his pocket and places it on the table. The waitress can't hold back her curiosity any longer. "Excuse me, sir. How do you manage to always come up with the exact change out of your pocket every time?"

"Well," says the man, "several years ago I was cleaning the attic and I found an old lamp. When I rubbed it, a genie appeared and offered me two wishes. My first wish was that if I ever had to pay for anything, I could just put my hand in my pocket, and the right amount of money would always be there."

"That's brilliant!" says the waitress. "Most people would wish for a million dollars or something, but you'll always be as rich as you want for as long as you live!"

"That's right! Whether it's a gallon of milk or a Rolls Royce, the exact money is always there," says the man.

The waitress asks, "One other thing, sir, what's with the ostrich?"

The man sighs and answers, "My second wish was for a tall chick with long legs, who agrees with everything I say."

**73. Don't pretend you're pregnant.** *(As soon as he learns that you're not, he's out of there.)*

**74. Don't invent another boyfriend to make him jealous.** *(Again, games are for kids.)*

**75. Don't keep insisting that he buy you things.** *(That's why you have a job and make your own money.)*

**76. Don't beg him to marry you.** *(Guys can smell a desperate, needy woman from a mile away.)*

# The Third Affair

A mortician was working late one night. It was his job to examine the dead bodies before they were sent off to be buried or cremated. As he examined the body of Mr. Gumbs, who was about to be cremated, he made an amazing discovery. Gumbs had the longest private part he had ever seen! "I'm sorry, Mr. Gumbs," said the mortician, "but I can't send you off to be cremated with a tremendously huge private part like this. It has to be saved for posterity."

With that, the coroner used his tools to remove the dead man's penis. He stuffed his prize into a briefcase and took it home. The first person he showed it to was his wife. "I have something to show you that you won't believe," he said, and opened up his briefcase.

"Oh my God!" his wife screamed. "Gumbs is dead!"

**77. Be financially responsible.** *(Don't expect him to pay your bills.)*

**78. Learn how to cook.** *(The shortest way to a man's heart is through his stomach.)*

**79. Don't befriend his family unless he invites you to.** *(If his family likes you, it doesn't mean he will like you any more than he already does.)*

**80. Appreciate the small things he does.** *(The small things eventually add up to big things.)*

# Be Strong, Honey

A prisoner escapes from his prison, where he had been kept for fifteen years. As he runs away, he finds a house and breaks into it looking for money and guns, but he finds a young couple in bed. He orders the guy out of bed and ties him up on a chair.

While tying the girl up to the bed, he gets on top of her, kisses her on the neck, then gets up and goes to the bathroom. While he is in there, the husband tells his wife: "Listen, this guy is an escaped prisoner, look at his clothes! He probably hasn't seen a naked woman in years. I saw how he kissed your neck. If he wants sex, don't resist, don't complain, just do what he tells you, give him satisfaction. This guy must be dangerous. If he gets angry, he may kill us. Be strong, honey. I love you."

To which the wife responds, "He was not kissing my neck, he was whispering in my ear. He told me he was gay and found you very sexy. Asked if we kept any Vaseline in the bathroom. Be strong, honey. I love you too..."

**81. Listen, don't interrupt.** *(Quit cutting him off to get your point in. He's only been talking for two minutes; you've probably talked for twenty.)*

**82. Stop nagging him!** *(This turns a man off every time you do it.)*

**83. Treat your man like a king, and he will treat you like a queen.** *(Go for the Oscar.)*

**84. Be honest.** *(No one likes a liar!)*

# Sisters of St. Francis

A man is driving down a deserted stretch of highway when he notices a sign out of the corner of his eye. It reads: *Sisters of St. Francis House of Prostitution, ten miles ahead.*

He thinks it was a figment of his imagination and drives on without a second thought. Soon he sees another sign, which says: *Sisters of St. Francis House of Prostitution, five miles ahead.*

Suddenly, he begins to realize that these signs are for real. Then he drives past a third sign saying: *Sisters of St. Francis House of Prostitution, next right.*

His curiosity gets the best of him, and he pulls into the drive. On the far side of the parking lot is a stone building with a small sign next to the door reading: *Sisters of St. Francis.* He climbs the steps and rings the bell. The door is answered by a nun in a long black habit, who asks, "What may we do for you, my son?" He answers, "I saw your signs along the highway and was interested in possibly doing business."

"Very well, my son. Please follow me."

He is led through many winding passages and is soon quite disoriented. The nun stops at a closed door and tells the man, "Please knock on this door." He does as he is told, and another nun in a long habit, holding a tin cup, answers the door. This nun instructs, "Please place $100 in the cup, then go through the large wooden door at the end of this hallway." He gets $100 out of his wallet and places it in the second nun's cup.

He trots eagerly down the hall and slips through the door, pulling it shut behind him. As the door locks behind him, he finds himself back in the parking lot, facing another small sign: *Go in peace. You have just been screwed by the Sisters of St. Francis. Serves you right, you sinner.*

**85. Don't show up to his house unannounced.** *(Unless you want your feelings hurt, don't do it.)*

**86. Know what you want. Think your own thoughts; have your own opinions and your own career.** *(Men like a woman who has a plan and goals for the future, not a woman who is just coasting through life reacting to the world around her.)*

**87. Be adventurous with sex. Change positions and places.** *(Nothing raises the passion like doing it in a hotel elevator at 2 AM as you ascend fifty floors to your room.)*

**88. Learn how to do a lap dance or a strip tease for your man.** *(This is the surest way to keep him out of the strip clubs. If you're really good at it, he might tip you big money.)*

# Dinner

A newly wed wife is determined to be the perfect mate to her man, so on their first day as husband and wife, she spends most of the day in the kitchen and prepares a meal for him that would befit a king. The husband arrives home from work, looks at the food, and says, "Honey, the food looks wonderful, but what I really want is sex."

Trying to be the perfect wife, off to the bedroom she goes. The next day, she again cooks a seven-course meal for her hard working husband. On arriving home the second evening, he again looks at the food and says, "Honey, it looks great, but what I really need is sex!" With no questions asked, it's off to the bedroom they go.

On the third evening, the husband comes home to a bizarre sight. He sees his wife stark naked, sliding down the banister. Dazed and confused, he asks her what she was doing. She boldly replies, "Nothing much, just heating up your dinner."

**89. Get a sense of humor.** *(Don't take yourself too seriously. You're replaceable—just like the next lady.)*

**90. Respect his privacy.** *(Looking through his cell phone history to see who he is calling is a big red flag that you're psycho.)*

**91. Don't fish for compliments.** *(If the new dress you are wearing looks nice, he will tell you. Quit asking him constantly if he likes your new dress, hairdo, make-up, etc.)*

**92. Keep a clean house.** *(Cleanliness is next to godliness).*

# Four Little Animals

A teacher asked her class, "What do you want out of life?"

A little girl in the back row raised her hand and said, "All I want out of life is four little animals."

The teacher asked, "Really? And what four little animals would that be, sugar?"

The little girl answered, "A mink on my back, a Jaguar in the garage, a tiger in the bed, and a jackass to pay for all of it."

# The Fourth Affair

A woman was in bed with her lover when she heard her husband opening the front door. "Hurry," she said, "stand in the corner." Then she quickly rubbed baby oil all over him and then dusted him with talcum powder. "Don't move until I tell you to," she whispered. "Just pretend you're a statue."

"What's this, honey?" the husband inquired as he entered the room. "Oh, it's a statue," she replied nonchalantly. "The Smith's bought one for their bedroom. I liked it so much, I got one for us too."

No more was said about the statue, not even later when they went to sleep. Around two in the morning, the husband got out of bed, went to the kitchen, and returned a while later with a sandwich and a glass of milk. "Here," he said to the statue, "eat something. I stood like an idiot at the Smith's for three days and nobody offered me as much as a glass of water."

**93. Send him cards and thank-you notes.** *(Men like to be romanced, just like women do.)*

**94. Wait for him to invite you to holiday events with his family.** *(Don't just invite yourself.)*

**95. Say what you mean and mean what you say.** *(Don't tell him you want to be in a relationship today and two weeks later that you just want to be friends.)*

**96. Don't get advice about guys from other women.** *(If you want to know about men, ask another man.)*

# $500

A woman was walking down the street when a man approached her. The man said, "I must have you right now! I'll drop $500 on the ground at your feet, and in the time it takes for you to pick it up, I can have my way with you from behind!"

The woman thought it over and told the man to wait a minute. She called her girlfriend on her cell phone and told her about the man's proposition. Her girlfriend said "When he drops the $500 on the ground, I'm sure you can pick it up and run before he gets his pants down. Call me back and tell me what happened."

An hour and a half later, the lady called her girlfriend back. "What happened?" the girlfriend asked.

The lady said, "That asshole had $500 in quarters!"

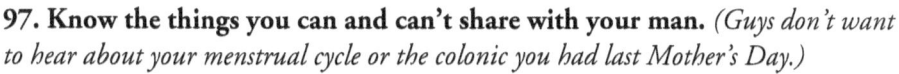

**97. Know the things you can and can't share with your man.** *(Guys don't want to hear about your menstrual cycle or the colonic you had last Mother's Day.)*

**98. Don't leave your things at his place without asking him first.** *(Leaving your tampons under his bathroom sink or hanging your stockings up in his bathroom are no-nos!)*

**99. Go to church.** *(Don't wait for him to ask you.)*

**100. Don't call your ex for help of any kind.** *(This is the ultimate slap in the face to a guy.)*

# God Bless Mommy

A father put his three-year-old daughter to bed, told her a story, and listened to her prayers, which she ended by saying, "God bless Mommy, God bless Daddy, God bless Grandma, and good-bye, Grandpa."

The father asked, "Why did you say 'Good-bye Grandpa?'"

The little girl said, "I don't know, Daddy, it just seemed like the thing to do." The next day, her grandpa died.

The father thought it was a strange coincidence. A few months later, the father put the girl to bed and listened to her prayers, which went like this: "God bless Mommy, God bless Daddy, and good-bye, Grandma." The next day, the grandmother died. Several weeks later, when the girl was going to bed, the dad heard her say, "God bless Mommy and good-bye, Daddy." He practically went into shock. He couldn't sleep all night and got up at the crack of dawn to go to his office. He was nervous as a cat all day, had lunch sent in, and watched the clock.

He figured if he could get by until midnight he would be okay. He felt safe in the office, so instead of going home at the end of the day, he stayed there, drinking coffee, looking at his watch, and jumping at every sound. Finally midnight arrived, and he breathed a sigh of relief and went home. When he got home, his wife said, "I've never seen you work so late. What's the matter?" He said, "I've just spent the worst day of my life, and I don't want to talk about it."

She said, "You think you had a bad day! You'll never believe what happened to me. This morning the mailman dropped dead on our porch."

**101. Be consistent.** *(Nothing drives a man crazier than a wishy-washy woman who can't make up her mind.)*

**102. Don't hint about moving in together. Let it be his idea.** *(Men like their space so be respectful of it.)*

**103. Don't try to run his career.** *(Unless you're his agent or manager, stay out of his business unless he asks you.)*

**104. Provide condoms some of the time.** *(The responsibility is both of yours, not just his.)*

# Marital Bliss

A typical macho man married a typical good-looking lady, and after the wedding, he laid down the following rules:

"I'll be home when I want, if I want, and at what time I want, and I don't expect any hassle from you. I expect a great dinner to be on the table unless I tell you that I won't be home for dinner. I'll go hunting, fishing, boozing, and card playing when I want with my old buddies, and don't you give me a hard time about it. Those are my rules. Any comments?"

His new bride said, "No, that's fine with me. Just understand that there will be sex here at 7:00 every night whether you're here or not."

**105. Learn to forgive.** *(Holding on to grudges isn't good for any relationship or your health.)*

**106. Don't ask him to give up sports.** *(This is like asking a man to stop breathing. It's not happening, so forget about it.)*

**107. Have a best friend who you can tell your deepest, darkest secrets too.** *(Some revelations could drive a wedge into your relationship.)*

**108. Keep up with current events and world news.** *(It makes for healthy conversation in a relationship.)*

## Bitter Quarrel

A husband and wife have a bitter quarrel on the day of their fortieth wedding anniversary. The husband yells, "When you die, I'm getting you a headstone that reads: 'Here Lies My Wife—Cold as Ever.'"

"Yeah?" she replies. "When you die, I'm getting you a headstone that reads: 'Here Lies My Husband—Stiff at Last.'"

## No Good in Bed

A husband (a doctor) and his wife are having a fight at the breakfast table. The husband gets up in a rage and says, "And you are no good in bed either," and storms out of the house. After some time, he realizes he was nasty and decides to make amends, so he rings her up. She comes to the phone after many rings. The irritated husband says, "What took you so long to answer the phone?"

She says, "I was in bed."

Her husband asks, "In bed this early? Doing what?"

She says, "Getting a second opinion!"

**109. Learn to play sports that your man is into.** *(The couple that plays together stays together.)*

**110. Be punctual!** *(There is no such thing as C.P.T.—colored people time.)*

**111. Don't tell your man every time someone hits on you.** *(We know there are other people who find you attractive.)*

**112. Don't have public arguments.** *(What you do in public, you will do at home.)*

## Grab My Breasts

A woman went into a department store and told the clerk that she wanted to return a toaster for a refund because it didn't work. The clerk told her that he couldn't give her a refund because she bought it on special.

All of a sudden, the woman threw her arms up and yelled, "Grab my breasts! Grab my breasts!" The clerk didn't know what to do, so he called the store manager, who asked her if he could help. She explained that she wanted to return the nonworking toaster for a refund, and he told her that he would not give her a refund because she bought the toaster on special.

Once again, she yelled, "Grab my breasts! Grab my breasts!" The manager was taken aback and asked her why she was yelling that particular phrase. She replied, "Because I like my breasts grabbed when I'm getting screwed!"

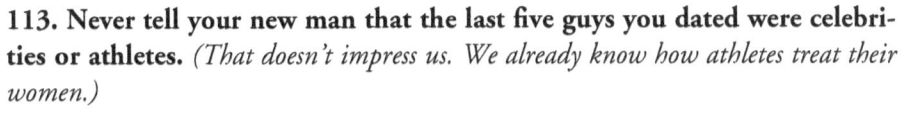

**113. Never tell your new man that the last five guys you dated were celebrities or athletes.** *(That doesn't impress us. We already know how athletes treat their women.)*

**114. Stop telling him about your past.** *(Some things are best not discussed.)*

**115. Don't offer advice unless it is requested.** *(If you don't have anything nice to say, don't say anything at all.)*

**116. Make sure your friends and family members respect your man.** *(Manners and respect carry you a long way in life.)*

# The Nun

A San Francisco cabby picks up a nun. She gets into the cab, and the driver won't stop staring at her in the rearview mirror. She asks him why he is staring, and he replies, "I have a question to ask you, but I don't want to offend you."

She answers, "My dear son, you cannot offend me. When you're as old as I am and have been a nun as long as I have, you get a chance see and hear just about everything. I'm sure that there's nothing you could say or ask that I would find offensive."

"Well, I've always had a fantasy about kissing a nun."

She responds, "Well, let's see what we can do about that: Number One: You have to promise you are single. Number Two: You must be Catholic."

The cab driver is very excited and says, "Yes, I am single, and I'm Catholic too!"

"OK," the nun says, "pull into the next alley." He does, and the nun fulfills his fantasy with a kiss that would make a hooker blush.

Once they get back on the road, the cab driver starts crying. "My dear child," says the nun, "why are you crying?"

"Forgive me, Sister, but I have sinned. I lied, I must confess—I'm married and I'm Jewish."

The nun says, "That's OK, my name is Kevin and I'm on my way to a Halloween party."

**117. When you are out, be sure to introduce your man to everyone you run into.** *(Especially the ones you give a big hug.)*

**118. Our business is our business.** *(Don't call your ex for advice about your current relationship.)*

**119. Never tell your man that he is doing too much for his mother.** *(This is grounds for divorce.)*

**120. Talking about past relationships is a big turnoff.** *(He doesn't want to hear about your ex-boyfriends or-husbands. That's what your girlfriends are for.)*

# New Wives

Three men were sitting together bragging about how they had set their new wives straight on their duties.

The first man had married a woman from Pennsylvania and bragged that he had told his wife she was going to do all the dishes and house cleaning that needed to be done at their house. He said that it took a couple days, but on the third day, he came home to a clean house and dishes that were all washed and put away.

The second man had married a woman from West Virginia. He bragged that he had given his wife orders that she was to do all the cleaning, dishes, and cooking. He told them that the first day he didn't see any results, but the next day it was better. By the third day, his house was clean, the dishes were done, and he had a huge dinner on the table.

The third man had married an island girl. He boasted that he told her his house was to be cleaned, dishes washed, the cooking done, and laundry washed. And this was all to be her responsibility. He said the first day he didn't see anything, and the second day he didn't see anything, but by the third day some of the swelling had gone down so he could see a little out of his left eye!

**121. Stay out of Internet chat rooms.** *(Cyber sex is cheating!)*

**122. Give him space and stop being clingy.** *(You're his lady, not a piece of lint.)*

**123. Get a hobby.** *(This makes for a healthier relationship.)*

**124. Cook his favorite meal for him once in a while.** *(Spaghetti doesn't count, nor does making reservations.)*

## The Sixth Affair

Jake was dying. His wife, Becky, was maintaining a candlelight vigil by his side. She held his fragile hand, tears running down her face. Her praying roused him from his slumber. He looked up, and his pale lips began to move slightly.

"Becky, my darling," he whispered.

"Hush, my love," she said. "Rest, don't talk."

He was insistent. "Becky," he said in his tired voice, "I have something that I must confess."

"There's nothing to confess," replied the weeping Becky, everything's all right, go to sleep."

"No, no, I must die in peace. Becky, I slept with your sister, your best friend, her best friend, and your mother!"

"I know, my sweet one," whispered Becky, "let the poison work."

**125. Don't hold grudges.** *(Deal with the problem and move on.)*

**126. Look appealing**. *(Just because you have him doesn't mean you have to stop looking good. There is plenty more eye candy out there.)*

**127. Stop gossiping**. *(Nobody likes a gossiper but another gossiper.)*

**128. Keep your family out of your relationship.** *(Too many cooks spoil the pot.)*

# Airline Passenger

An airline's passenger cabin was being served by an obviously gay flight attendant, who seemed to put everyone into a good mood as he served them food and drinks.

As the plane prepared to descend, he came swishing down the aisle and announced to the passengers, "Captain Huggins has asked me to announce that he'll be landing the big scary plane shortly, lovely people, so if you could just put up your trays, that would be super."

On his trip back up the aisle, he noticed that a well-dressed, rather exotic-looking woman hadn't moved a muscle. "Perhaps you didn't hear me over those big brute engines. I asked you to raise your trazy-poo so the main man can pitty-pat us on the ground."

She calmly turned her head and said, "In my country, I am called a princess. I take orders from no one." to which the flight attendant replied without missing a beat, "Well, sweet cheeks, in my country, I'm called a queen, so I outrank you...Tray up, bitch!

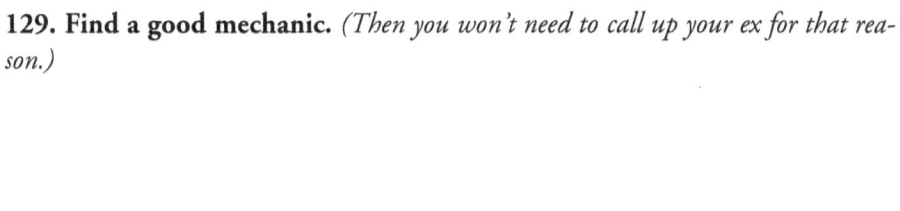

**129. Find a good mechanic.** *(Then you won't need to call up your ex for that reason.)*

**130. Don't tell him how to raise his kids from a previous relationship.** *(Silence can be golden at times.)*

**131. Help him around the house.** *(Fix things, move furniture, clean, and cook).*

**132. Don't expect him to be God.** *(There is no such thing as a perfect man, so deal with it.)*

## Marriage and the Math Lesson

After many years of marriage, a professor of mathematics sent a fax to his wife. It read:

Dear Wife:

You must realize that you are fifty-four years old, and I have certain needs, which you are no longer able to satisfy. I am otherwise happy with you as a wife, and I sincerely hope you will not be hurt or offended to learn that by the time you receive this letter, I will be at the Grand Hotel with my eighteen-year-old teaching assistant. I'll be home before midnight.

Your Husband

When he arrived at the hotel, there was a faxed letter waiting for him that read as follows:

Dear Husband:

You, too, are fifty-four years old, and by the time you receive this letter, I will be at the Breakwater Hotel with the eighteen-year-old pool boy. Being the brilliant mathematician that you are, you can easily appreciate the fact that eighteen goes into fifty-four a lot more times than fifty-four goes into eighteen.

Don't wait up.

Sincerely,
Your Wife

**133. Trust him.** *(If you can't, then leave him alone.)*

**134. Do not confide in his mother.** *(There is an old saying: "Water and oil don't mix.")*

**135. Never use crying to manipulate him.** *(Manipulation only works for so long.)*

**136. Quit playing the victim when things don't go your way.** *(Stand up and be accountable for your actions.)*

# Psychiatric Session

A psychiatrist was conducting a group therapy session with four young mothers and their small children. "You all have obsessions," he observed.

To the first mother, he said, "You are obsessed with eating. You've even named your daughter Candy."

He turned to the second mom. "Your obsession is money. Again, it manifests itself in your child's name, Penny."

He turned to the third mom. "Your obsession is alcohol. Again, it manifests itself in your child's name, Champagne."

At this point, the fourth mother got up, took her little boy by the hand, and whispered, "Come on, Dick, let's go."

**137. Learn to deal with your insecurities.** *(Again, seek professional help if you have to.)*

**138. Keep your quality friends, because you'll need them in the bad times.** *(A friend indeed will always help a friend in need.)*

**139. Don't try to boss him around.** *(Men hate to be told what to do. Instead of telling, suggest.)*

**140. Stop whining about every little thing.** *(Choose the most important, life-changing things to complain about, and let the small stuff go.)*

# Blond Husband

After having their eleventh child, a blond couple decided that they had had enough children because they could not afford a larger bed. So the blond husband went to his doctor and told him that he and his wife didn't want to have any more children.

The doctor told him there was a procedure called a vasectomy that would fix the problem but it was expensive. A less costly alternative was to go home, get a firework, light it, put it in a beer can, then hold the can up to his ear and count to ten.

The blond husband said to the doctor, "I may not be the smartest guy in the world, but I don't see how putting a firework in a beer can next to my ear is going to help me."

"Trust me, it will do the job," said the doctor.

So the blond husband went home, lit a banger, and put it in a beer can. He held the can up to his ear and began to count: "One, two, three, four, five," at which point he paused and placed the beer can between his legs so he could continue counting on his other hand.

**141. Don't ask him to buy feminine products.** *(Men don't want their buddies to think they are sissies.)*

**142. Don't question him about his ex-girlfriends.** *(What you don't know won't hurt you.)*

**143. Let him dress himself some of the time.** *(At least when you're not going out with him.)*

**144. Get a life.** *(Your life will be a lot fuller when you do meet a man.)*

## What Does a Kiss Taste Like?

One day, a teacher had a taste test with her students. She picked a little boy to do the first test. She blindfolded him, put a Hershey kiss in his mouth, and asked, "Do you know what this is?"

"No, I don't," said the little boy.

"Okay, I'll give you a clue. It's the thing your daddy wants from your mom before he goes to work."

Suddenly, a little girl at the back of the room yelled, "Spit it out! It's a piece of ass!"

## The Lottery

A woman wins forty million dollars in the state lottery. She calls her husband on the phone and says, "Honey, I just won forty million dollars in the lottery. Pack your bags."

Her husband was so excited, he asked, "Are we going somewhere warm or somewhere cold? I need to know so I can pack the right clothes."

The wife replied, "I don't care what you pack, just get the hell out!"

# Afterword

Although men and women think differently, neither sex can live without the other. For too long, women have searched high and low trying to find out what men really want. Hopefully this book has given many of you women an inside peek at how a man really thinks and the key to unlocking his heart. Keep the faith and don't stop loving. There is true love out there for everyone.

# About the Authors

**Denver Williams**—(left) An accomplished actor who has appeared in numerous feature films and television series, including *Arlington Road, Walker Texas Ranger,* and *Unsolved Mysteries,* and as host of *BET Group Therapy.* He has also appeared in several television commercials, including those for Toy 'R' Us, Toyota, and Lockheed Martin.

**Jeff Hodge**—(right) A fifteen-year stand-up comedian who has appeared in the feature films *Crocodile Dundee in LA* and *Deuce Bigalow: Male Gigolo.* He has served as a writer for George Lopez, Arsenio Hall, and *The Steve Harvey Radio Show.* Jeff has also written several humorous books, including *101+ Ways to Get Out of a Traffic Ticket.* For more information on Jeff, visit his Website: <u>www.jeffhodge.com</u>.

# Other Books by Jeff Hodge

*101+ Ways to Get Out f a Traffic Ticket*—$10.00—A humorous book filled with lots of funny excuses and stories motorists have used over the years to get out of traffic tickets.

ISBN: 0-9633347-0-0

*Pet Peeves: Things That Tick Me Off About Driving*—$10.00—A humorous book that shows motorists how to deal with their pet peeves and road rage when they are behind the wheel.

ISBN: 0-9633347-5-1

*101 Ways to Stay Awake When on the Road*—$10.00—A humorous book that has funny takes on road signs and what they mean. It also gives readers creative ways to stay awake when they find themselves falling asleep behind the wheel.

ISBN: 0-9633347–1-9

Order your **autographed** copies now. Visit www.jeffhodge.com for more details or simply use the order form on the following page.

# *Order Form*

Name: _____

Address: _____

City: _____State: _____Zip: _____

-------------------------------------------------------------------------------

Name of title: _____

Number of copies _____      *      Price:        _____

                                    Subtotal:     _____

Shipping & Handling:                $3.50

                                    Total:        _____

Make money orders payable to: **Yeah Mon Entertainment** * P.O. Box 88304 * Los Angeles, CA 90009-8304. Please allow 4–6 for weeks delivery.

978-0-595-37633-9
0-595-37633-9